TEXAS OUT BACK

TEXAS

Sketches by Harry Anthony DeYoung

OUT BACK

Text by Leon Hale

MADRONA PRESS, INC. / AUSTIN, TEXAS

ISBN 0-89052-002-X

Library of Congress Catalogue Card No. 73–89806
Copyright © 1973 by Anita DeYoung Ischar
All Rights Reserved

Second Printing 1975
Third Printing 1975
Fourth Printing 1979

Manufactured in the United States of America

CONTENTS

*When a man reproached him for go-
ing into unclean places, he said,
"The sun too penetrates into privies,
but is not polluted by them."*
Diogenes

PUBLISHER'S NOTE

NOT SO MANY YEARS AGO, indoor plumbing was foreign to a large percentage of American homes. In its place were well rope and bucket, washstand and basin, a galvanized tub for bathing, a tea kettle on the woodburning kitchen range—and the little house out back.

Many of the trappings of the era that preceded "modern conveniences" have found their way into antique shops. Some are recalled by artistic representation. Yet one vital part of this vanishing Americana has been largely neglected—the outhouse.

Families who had to put up with an outdoor "facility" longer than they desired often regarded it with disdain. This typical attitude is expressed by Bill Davenport of Austin: "Ours came down the day we got our inside bathroom. We wanted to be done with it forever."

But in the contemplation of the past and the manner of life in yesteryear, how can one ignore the privy?

With this thought Madrona Press proudly presents these sketches by Harry Anthony DeYoung. The outstanding pencil drawings are offered for their artistic merit, and for the graphic story they tell of one facet of the American scene, now all but vanished.

Unfortunately, only the general locality of each sketch subject is known, and in some cases not even that much. The publisher is indebted to Mr. DeYoung's widow and their daughter, Mrs. Anita Ischar, for the information they were able to provide.

INTRODUCTION TO
THE SKETCHES

WHEN A MAN IS ASKED, for the first time, to write a piece for a book, he counts it an honor and wants to tell all his friends. So I told mine, and they asked, "What *kind* of book?" And I answered, "A book of privy sketches. Drawings. Of outdoor toilets." A few of the friends grinned and said, "Aw, come on." Some left me a weak "Oh," before they nodded slowly and turned away. A couple of them laughed coarsely. And one said, "Well, I can see why they picked *you*."

I was afraid to ask what that last remark meant. I decided to believe it meant that in past sentences I've written the outhouse has appeared often enough to indicate I'm at least not shy about the subject. That much is surely so. I consider the privy a significant cultural symbol. I think it symbolizes a long and waning chapter of American life, in a special way that no other man-built structure ever has. If I tried to pretend I'm too sophisticated to help put together a privy book, that would be such a sin that all Heaven's angels would weep in unison. It would be, as we used to say, going back on my raising. The summer song of the privy dirt dauber, the riffle of the catalog pages in a winter wind coming under the door—these things are etched deep in the record of my early times, and I cannot deny them.

I don't doubt there'll be those with the lofty notion that a privy sketchbook represents the pursuit of indignity. Nonsense, I say. I personally see a great deal of dignity in these fine sketches of Harry DeYoung. In certain ones of the privies themselves I find more dignity than I can see in most of the contemporary commercial buildings that keep springing up along big-city freeways. These drawings have artistic merit of the highest order.

Their examination brings one obvious question: Why would an artist with the reputation and talent of Harry Anthony DeYoung spend so much time drawing, in such handsome detail, twenty-one privies that he knew? I have no pat answer. If I could draw, and if I had drawn them, I could write you a book on why I did it. I would say that I am magnetized by disappearing things, that they pull me toward them, implore me to rescue memories of the times they represent.

If this sort of feeling was inside DeYoung when he sketched the privies, I do not know about it. It might have been. The drawings were made, most of them, in the early 1930's when the privy already was well into its decline. Perhaps DeYoung told himself, "The privy is fading from the American scene, and nobody is drawing privies, so I will draw them and preserve this vanishing Americana."

He never wrote any such sentiment down, if he had it. Nor expressed it orally to his close associates known to me, and these include his widow and his daughter.

The daughter is Anita DeYoung Ischar of San Antonio. She says, "I think he drew the privies as a fun thing. And also as a challenge, to see if he could capture the detail, the intricacy he saw in them. But he had a tremendous sense of humor."

I think probably there's the key, that it was a fun thing. No matter what high purpose might motivate an artist to produce art, when he's drawing twenty-one privies he's got to be grinning. Because a privy is just funny, and there is nothing you can do about it. I've made tests. I've had friends in the car, going down the highway, and I've pointed and

10

said, "Hey, lookit that ol' privy out there, listing to port." They've never failed to say, "Yeah!" And then laugh, at least a little. I can't tell you why, not in one sweeping statement. I've thought myself dizzy about why, and made a list of a dozen reasons, some of which would embarrass me to write down, so I leave them out. It's best just to acknowledge that a privy is funny. It's one of the few things I can think of that can be funny just by reason of its existence, just by standing out there at the end of a path.

A careful study of James Whitcomb Riley's famous poem "The Passing of the Outhouse" (a copy of which graces my office wall) convinces me that it's mighty difficult to treat a privy with total seriousness. I suspect Riley meant to try it, when he started out. The poem has a total of thirty-two lines. The poet got past the first ten of them with a straight face, writing of memories, of worn paths, of swinging doors and simple architecture and buzzing flies and web-spinning spiders. But then he couldn't stand it any longer and at the eleventh and twelfth lines he threw in:

"And once a swarm of hornets bold, had built a palace
there,
And stung my unsuspecting aunt—I must not tell you
where."

After that Riley kept on being funny all the way to the end.

One day, during the deeps of the Depression, Harry De-Young was driving through the Hill Country in the Boerne area, and spotted an outhouse he liked the look of. So he stopped and got out and began to sketch it. Pretty soon a woman came out of the house that the privy served. A Mexican-American woman who had no English. Seeing DeYoung was an artist, she sign-languaged that she'd like him to sketch her portrait. He spoke no Spanish but he sign-languaged back that he wasn't interested in doing her portrait, that he only wanted to sketch her privy. I consider it a credit to that lady's character that she ended up lying across a cypress log, suffering a fit of laughter that the first artist who'd stopped at her home had come to draw the toilet.

You see how that anecdote demonstrates that a privy can be funny without trying. If DeYoung had come to paint the house, the barn, the well, the livestock, the wildflowers— would that have been funny? Why, no.

That little story, told by his widow and daughter, also provides a peek inside Harry DeYoung. He had to be not only a man of good humor but one of high self-confidence and considerable courage. When he was drawing the privies he was not what you could call a young artist struggling for recognition. He had been an instructor at the National Academy of Art, recognized as one of the top pencil artists in the country. His painting, as well, had drawn acclaim, particularly in the Chicago area. I say it takes a confident man to let himself be seen drawing outhouses when he had already painted pictures hanging in high places. He was laughed at, many times, for producing his privy art, and it does require courage to keep doing what observers are poking fun at.

I picture DeYoung drawing privies and grinning, while the others laughed, but I'd have to say his sketches come the closest I've seen to a serious treatment of the subject. Oh, they do comment. I see a quiet humor in some, gentle chuckles in others. But I can't find any nasty jokes; I don't get any guffaws; none of what we've come to call outhouse humor. This is earnest art, full of respect and love and gentle smiles. I've searched it, sheet by sheet, for caricature, satire, travesty, spoof, lampoon, or parody. I find none.

Now then, let's clear up this one thing, about vanishing Americana. Vanishing, yes; going, going . . . but not gone. Not yet. On the twenty-first day of June, 1973, I sat in the only cafe in the little town of Clemville, in Matagorda County. Just waiting on dinner time. Talking to Harry Cowger, whose wife Dee operates that cafe. I hadn't been in the place before. When it came hand-washing time, I made a weak little joke by asking Dee Cowger if her cafe had indoor plumbing. Straight-faced as a statue she said, "No, but if you'll step right across the blacktop and walk between the post office and the garage and turn right at the butane tank, you'll find a privy back there against the hedge."

Then she laughed, because it's no longer possible to give directions to an outhouse without laughing. But Dee was serious about the privy—it's there, and is used daily, so we mustn't say that the privy is gone, because it's not. I'd guess thousands yet stand in Texas alone. I see them most frequently in the ragged ends of small towns, but I don't doubt they exist also in city slums. Most are no longer used, at least not for the original purpose, and mighty few I see are maintained. So we have come to expect a privy to be in disrepair, to be leaning, to have a sagging door, to be a stranger to a paint brush.

I have personal knowledge of three *new* privies, built in the last five years. True, they don't serve residences. Two are on hunting leases and the third is at a fish camp, where it represents luxury just as the very first outhouse ever built did. I know one fine privy that stands somewhere between Cotulla and Artesia Wells in the Texas Brush Country. A handsome structure built on piers and equipped with steps. It's half as high as a windmill tower and doubles as a deer stand and is called, by those who climb its steps, the High-Rise.

Any man who loves and frequents rural taverns, as I do, will snort at the suggestion that privies have all settled into the past. In just the last decade I've met a lot of nice people along the paths that lead away from the back doors of Texas country taverns. I wonder if you'd believe this —that an outhouse actually saved my favorite tavern from burning to the earth. Would you like to hear how?

Scheller's Place is in Glen Flora, tiny little town on the

13

lower Colorado River, in that flat coast country between Houston and Corpus Christi. For fifteen years I've gathered there regularly with friends, to cut up old scores, to sing songs, to swap stories.

I love that place. Some day it will pass away and be no more, and if that happens before my own time comes, I will cry out in grief. I will smite the earth, and water it with my tears.

That very tragedy almost happened in the spring of 1972.

Ed Scheller, bless the memory of him, never would install an indoor restroom in his tavern. He was opposed to it on the grounds, first, that it was expensive, and, second, that it didn't seem to him entirely sanitary for people to be going to the bathroom right there under the same roof where they were sipping suds.

So he maintained privies out back, separate and almost equal. The one for the ladies was the last outhouse I know of in Texas to be stolen on Halloween, hauled away, and parked on somebody's front lawn.

In March of '72, Northington's Store in Glen Flora caught fire. The store is only three doors down Bridge Street from Scheller's, which houses what I consider to be one of the most entertaining museums in the Southwest. The relics covering Scheller's walls range from the cured hide of Ed's old alligator (which used to sleep inside by the stove in winter) to the pickled appendix of a prominent housewife from Wharton.

The fire in Northington's started late, after ten P.M., when the streets are sure not crowded. So it's a pure marvel that the blaze was detected early. If it hadn't been, the fire would have spread to Mabel Frankum's grocery store next door. And then through the washateria. And next to Scheller's. Possibly even to the post office beyond. But here's why it didn't: At ten-thirty, a customer in Scheller's walked out back to visit the privy, saw the flames, and reported the fire. Trucks from

14

six surrounding towns came and put it out. Do you see the point? If Ed Scheller had installed an indoor restroom in his tavern, nobody would have gone out to the privy, the fire wouldn't have been seen, and Glen Flora would have burned as sure as Chicago did.

I have tender feelings toward privies for reasons more deeply rooted in my past. Anybody of middle age who has logged time in the country must have similar recollections. Of Grandma slipping on the path and breaking a hip. Of the grass fire spreading to the outhouse and leveling it while the men were in the field, forcing all hands into the woods twice daily until a new privy could be built. Of your mother carefully tearing all the corset ads out of the mail-order catalog, so the boys wouldn't see the illustrations and become sex fiends.

The removal of the corset ads came about the time the oldest son in a family entered puberty. Not long afterward, he'd generally quit going to the privy. In West Texas, where I grew up, few boys past thirteen used the outhouse. I've heard evidence the same was true in East Texas. O.T. Baker of the Institute of Texan Cultures was reared "out from Center" in Shelby County, which is just about as East Texas as you can get. He has told me, "Using the privy was for women, and not a manly thing to do. The boys went to the barn."

Yes, but before graduating and going on toward the barn, youngsters laid up plenty of memories. My earliest, of an outhouse, is fear. I've always wondered whether Freud was able to keep from laughing the first time one of his patients confessed a childhood horror of falling through the hole. There were other fearsome prospects for a child. Black widow spiders. Stinging insects.

And snakes. Anybody who ever confronted even a half-grown chicken snake in the close quarters of a privy knows there's no such creature as a harmless serpent. One may be nonvenomous and still inspire a person to harm himself. A boy could get hurt seriously, trying to run with his overalls down around his ankles.

Then the fear of embarrassment, the dreadful thought that the latch would fail and the door would blow open and there you'd be, for the world to see and to laugh at. I remember privies with chains or ropes on the inside of their doors, so you could sit there and hold on. Gave you confidence. You could stage your own tug-of-war with the wind, or with another person on the outside, desperate to get in.

The privy could be a retreat, as well as a comfort station. Few families in outhouse times had private bedrooms where individuals could go and shut doors and be alone. The privy, then, provided at least a temporary place of privacy. A person could hide away there and be assured he'd not be issued an order or asked what he was about.

In town, the condition of outhouses was a clue to family status. I remember holding people in respect because their privy was whitewashed, or had a weather vane or a birdhouse on top, or had curtains over its little diamond-shaped windows, or had two doors, or had an impressive multiple-hole arrangement.

But to me the most curious reflection of all is that the privy, as it touched our lives, was a paradox and a contradiction. That is, it was an obvious and familiar and necessary part of the home scene; yet in a very strong sense it represented the Forbidden. The people I grew up among were mighty careful who was within earshot when they discussed sensitive matters, such as those pertaining to the privy, because it wasn't "nice." Those were people who were struggling under the severe moral code imposed upon them by their puritanical Bible-Belt forebears. They did not call a female dog a bitch. Nor a stallion a stud. Nor a bull a bull; called it a male instead. They wouldn't even say a woman was pregnant. Because words like stud and bull and bitch and pregnant were

16

suggestive and therefore Forbidden, at least in polite company. The "nice" thing to do about a privy was just to ignore it as Forbidden.

But it was hard to ignore. There it was, forever near, staring back at us with its one door-eye, evident as a big red barn, always there, to suggest Forbidden topics. Other Forbidden things could be hidden, but it was hard to hide an outhouse.

Because it was Forbidden, it often was disguised with euphemistic names in polite company. It was variously called closet, backhouse, johnny, Chic Sale (for the author of a book on privy building), and "the post office." It was dubbed the "Federal Building" by unreconstructed Rebels, "Congress" by political satirists. Down around Yoakum, one family privy was given a painted sign, like the railroad depot, proclaiming it "Fort Worth." One then could announce his destination without having to be crude about it.

Some of the most ridiculous, and most memorable, privy stories in our culture sprang out of man-woman situations. My friend Vernon Marie Schuder of Riverside, near Huntsville, can now laugh about the privy her husband built soon after she married him. He made the structure so weathertight and roomy that he used it to store his saddle. Then one day while he was away, a friend of his came to borrow the saddle. Mrs. Schuder was rendered absolutely ill from the embarrassment of having to tell where it was stored. Today a woman would say, "It's in the privy." And laugh, right? But forty years ago, a woman talking to a casual acquaintance about a privy was Forbidden.

I expect it would have been hard, in privy times, for a man and a woman to commit a greater trespass than to go into an outhouse at the same time. Mrs. Schuder contributes the following, which shows that some incidents that happened in privies were more tragic than funny:

"One of my in-law aunts used to talk about the time she was a student at a one-teacher school at Crabb's Prairie

(Walker County). The teacher was a man. My aunt and a friend were the two oldest girls in the school. One day they asked to be excused and went out to the privy.

"This friend of my aunt's wanted to show how limber and athletic she was, so she got down on the floor and managed to put both feet behind her head. Well, she couldn't get them down. My aunt tugged and twisted but couldn't get them down either. Finally she gave up and went for the teacher, who came out there and by sheer strength managed to get the legs unhooked.

"Do you know, that poor girl was so embarrassed she quit school and never got up the courage to return. So that incident in the privy ended her education."

My own most memorable privy story happened back in my green years in West Texas, when I used to attend country church services in the afternoon with a family named Foster. They had a boy near my age, and they had two big healthy daughters about fifteen and sixteen. The building where services were held was really an old frame schoolhouse.

There was always a lot of early arriving, and visiting, and standing around, waiting for church to begin. On this afternoon the weather was threatening, and it delivered. Just before church time, the skies erupted with a summer thunderstorm, a real tree-splitter and stump-floater. We were all hustled into the schoolhouse.

When heads were counted it was determined by Mrs. Foster that her two girls were missing. During the visiting hour they had gone to the privy on the back of the school ground and were stranded out there in the storm.

So a decision had to be made, whether to go ahead and start services or hold up long enough to rescue the Foster girls. The men got off in a group and mumbled, while the women appeared not to notice. It was bad enough to be discussing a Forbidden topic like a privy there in church, and to discuss it in a mixed group before children would have been unthinkable. A little bunch of us boys kept on the back row and stuffed the sleeves of our shirts in our mouths so our painful laughter couldn't be heard.

Finally it was decided not to do anything. Mr. Foster tiptoed to his wife, his expression solemn and pious, and whispered that if the storm got any worse they'd go out and get the girls. But for the present they would let them ride it out.

It hit me as a weak decision. I thought if the storm got any worse the outhouse would be gone, and the girls with it, because the wind was screaming and the thunder popping and the rain driving horizontal across the school yard. I have to count that my strangest thunderstorm—being there in church, standing up with a hymn book, listening to Scripture read and prayers said, and all the while one eye beamed out the window so I could be a witness when the outhouse blew away with the Foster girls.

That it didn't was a testimony to the craftsmanship of some long-dead carpenter. When the storm was over, here came the girls, strolling back up the path, calm as cream, trying to look as if they had sung every hymn and heard every prayer.

But to me the marvel is this: That on the way home, not a mention was made of the incident. Not a syllable. Just as if it never happened.

Before supper that night, the Foster girls confessed in private to their brother and me that the ordeal wasn't really so bad. Said the worst thing was the spiders, not the storm.

I never met Harry Anthony DeYoung. He died in 1956. But during the preparation of this material, I learned to admire him not only as an artist but also as a human being. One reason is, he once built a privy with his own talented hands. I learned that from his widow, who lives in San Antonio. He was teaching at Bailey's Harbor Summer School of Art in Wisconsin back during the 1920's and there on the shore of Lake Michigan he built a privy for his wife and daughter. I know artists who wouldn't stoop to privy building, or admit it if they ever had.

DeYoung was born in Chicago in 1893. When he came to Texas he was in his mid-thirties, and already had made a mark in the art world. He was a graduate of the University of Illinois and the Chicago Art Institute, as an honor student. He had a dozen years of teaching experience in the Midwest. His landscapes (oils) hung in several fine collections. But his art had, by the late 1920's, made him no more than a living.

In 1928 he moved to San Antonio, mainly in the hope that the change would improve his and his daughter's health. He had suffered a nervous breakdown, and his daughter was a sickly child. The family sold everything it owned except what could be put into an old touring car, and DeYoung brought his family to San Antonio.

He chose the Alamo City because a Texas wildflower-painting competition was based there at the time, and he had been urged to enter the contest. He was, principally, a landscape artist. San Antonio proved a happy choice for DeYoung because of a connection he made with Witte Museum, where he subsequently did much work. His murals may be seen there now, and in the city's St. Anthony Hotel also. He also was to do paintings to hang in the Alamo. One, quite famous, of Davy Crockett in the siege; and three portraits, of James Bonham, Dr. Amos Pollard, and Mrs. John Dickinson.

From the time he arrived in Texas in 1928 until his health failed in 1942, DeYoung was a teacher of art, either in studios in San Antonio or in summer art camps. He founded and directed DeYoung Painting Camp in the Davis Mountains and instructed at camps held in the Hill Country, the Big Bend area, and South Texas, at Port Isabel.

During their first years in Texas, the DeYoungs lived in the hills at Boerne and DeYoung commuted to his San Antonio classes. On weekends he would put his wife and daughter in the car and tour the back roads of the Boerne area, looking for sketch subjects. DeYoung developed a great love for the Hill Country, and for frontier culture. The privy drawing began on these family outings, in 1929. The latest date we have on any of the sketches is 1934. The majority of the little houses in this book are in the Boerne-Comfort area. Models for the remainder stood near Fort Davis. The Fort Davis privies are distinguished from the others by the sheet iron used in their construction, and by the absence of trees and native shrubbery.

Mrs. Ischar says now that a comparatively small amount of the time her father devoted to drawing and painting was spent on the privies. There is the temptation to speculate that he began it as a hobby, a sort of lark or relaxation. He was a man who found no reward in idleness.

"He was always sketching," Mrs. Ischar recalls. "He never just sat, without doing anything. He drew. If he went to a banquet, he would draw the whole time and end up with sketches of everybody at his table."

It would, of course, be interesting to have what comment DeYoung would care to make, now, on his privies. Perhaps he'd have none. The record is remarkably sparse on what he said, ever, about any of his paintings. We do know he disagreed that the Crockett in the Alamo was his finest work. His favorite picture, according to Mrs. DeYoung, is a forest snow scene in Illinois where he grew up. He also liked a huge mural in Witte Museum showing Indian Basket Makers at work.

Although wildflowers helped make a Texan of him, DeYoung would never paint bluebonnets for the obvious reason that they already had been overdone. He did a few portraits of living people but preferred not to, so Mrs. Ischar says, because the subjects almost always got angry at him. "That's because he would paint what he saw inside a person," his daughter says, "and not just the pretty face that was exposed."

In 1942, DeYoung had a stroke. His right side was paralyzed entirely. He was not yet fifty.

It seems characteristic of an artist who wouldn't paint bluebonnets, which were easy to sell, that he refused to give up his art. He taught himself to paint lefthanded, and painted that way until his death in 1956, at age sixty-two.

DeYoung spent his last thirteen years in the veterans' hospital in Waco, where he died. Those must have been heavy years for a man accustomed to laughing and working. There were disappointments. Few of his lefthand-painted pictures sold. He was dropped, following the stroke, from *Who's Who in America*. He lived to see the movie-inspired Davy Crockett boom, when prints of his Crockett painting in the Alamo sold well; but DeYoung received nothing because he had not retained reproduction rights to the painting. His income those last years was a monthly fifty-dollar World War I pension, and he was sending that to his wife in San Antonio.

DeYoung often expressed the wish to his family that his beloved privy drawings could somehow be published. So it is impossible to forego the wish that he could be with us now, to turn the pages that follow, and share our pleasure.

THE SKETCHES

Balcones Creek, Kendall County, is the site of this three-door privy that once served a rural school.

Initials adorn the face of this once-popular structure in the Boerne area which, at the time of the drawing, was serving principally to hold up the fence. The round louver is a classic feature.

27

Depression times are typified by the use of a cast-off storm shutter to form a wall of this neatly-built out-house. Location is the Boerne area.

29

Viney growth has taken over the walkway here, indicating this Boerne facility has been superseded by indoor plumbing or the building site abandoned. The barbwire fence in the background suggests a location at the edge of town.

Harry Anthony DeYoung
1932

While this *casita* appears to be in better condition than most, the overgrown walkway hints at scant use. In a rural setting, the site is near Boerne.

Though the trees appear different in these two sketches, the subject is the same. It served an unidentified school in the Boerne area. The undated second drawing, at right, shows the structure's deterioration since the first sketch was made in 1934.

Outhouses often were placed on the back corner of the lot, out of sight and smell. At this location between Boerne and Comfort, three lots seem to corner where the structures are.

The trellis of tree limbs in front of this privy near Welfare, Kendall County, evidently was intended to support a concealing growth of vine to blend the little house into the landscape and turn its ugliness into beauty.

Harry Anthony DeYoung
1934.

39

From the framework, it appears an ingenious work-
man built this backhouse in the Welfare area which,
like most of the country in the 1930's, had fallen on
hard times. Patching has been done with whatever
material was at hand. Large rocks are used to anchor
the roofing against a brisk wind. Perhaps the horse-
shoe over the door expresses the owner's longing for
prosperity's return.

41

Unique by its half stone, half board construction, this privy near Comfort apparently has been cast aside with the washboard that leans against the wall, symbolic of the transition to indoor plumbing. Stones from the fence in back apparently were appropriated to build the bottom half of the structure, providing protection from a northerly breeze.

43

Having rented his property near Waring (Kendall County) for summer art classes, the owner one day came upon the artist sketching his outhouse. "A man has to be crazy to paint a thing like that!" he exclaimed. DeYoung later did an oil painting of the birdhouse-adorned privy and gave it to the owner, remembered only as Mr. Angiers. Commented the recipient, "I never knew it looked so pretty."

The length of available boards evidently determined the manner of construction of this privy, sketched near Comfort in 1932. A spool nailed to the door serves as a handle.

Harry Anthony DeYoung
1932

47

This little house, also sketched near Comfort in 1932, has the traditional quarter-moon louver. The mesh fence suggests it was situated in the chicken yard.

49

On a ranch in far West Texas near Fort Davis, this privy was constructed of materials at hand by a builder who either did not own a saw or didn't want to blister his hands using it.

Sheet metal of unsuitable length and a couple of Nehi signs, prominent advertising pieces of the times, serve to stop holes in the sides of this structure in the sparsely populated Fort Davis area.

Looking upon an expansive view of mountains and stream, this crudely built structure near Fort Davis is seen from the rear.

Outhouse roofs usually were shed type or gabled; this specimen, with hip and gable, is distinctive. It stands out also for its adobe construction. Mountains in the background suggest the Fort Davis area.

While the construction method used here resembles that appearing most often in the sketches from the Fort Davis area, the trees and other surroundings are more typical of the Hill Country. The trees furnish support.

A sun visor has been added to the front of this privy which, in keeping with Chic Sale's *The Specialist*, occupies a spot adjacent to the woodpile.

Seen from behind a picket fence, distinctive features in this 1934 drawing are the birdhouse on top and the vent in the roof. The gate in the fence probably is the end of a piano crate.

63

This structure appears to be serving principally to support the birdhouse, since the ladder blocks the door. Altogether, four of the outhouse sketches show birdhouses on the roof, some of them possibly used to raise pigeons for the table.

Harry Anthony DeYoung.

65

Texas Out Back, the second book produced by Madrona Press, has been printed on Warren's No. 66 Antique Wove. Type used for text is eleven-point Waverley with two-point leading, set on Intertype by G&S Typesetters, Austin. Printing by offset lithography was done by Capital Printing Company of Austin.

Design by William A. Seymour

MADRONA PRESS, INC.
BOX 3750
AUSTIN, TEXAS 78764